KING*f*ISHER

Senior Editor
Belinda Weber

Editors
Mandy Cleeve, Jean Coppendale

Designer
Paul Griffin

Publishing Director
Chester Fisher

Authors
Nicola Baxter, Rosemary McCormick

Artwork Archivist
Wendy Allison

Assistant Artwork Archivist
Steve Robinson

KINGFISHER
Kingfisher Publications Plc
New Penderel House
283–288 High Holborn
London WC1V 7HZ

Published in hardback by Kingfisher Publications Plc
in 1996
Paperback edition published in 1998

ISBN 0 7534 0086 3 (hb)
10 9 8 7 6 5 4 3 2 1

ISBN 0 7534 0147 9 (pb)
10 9 8 7 6 5 4 3 2

A CIP catalogue record for this book is available from
the British Library.

Printed in Spain

Contents

British History

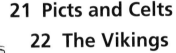

Around Britain

DENNIS the MENACE

HUMM!

CLICK!

SUPER-MARKET SWEEP!

MODERN BRITAIN'S NO PLACE FOR A MENACE, GNASHER!

LET'S BUILD A BRONZE AGE SETTLEMENT!

FIRST, WE NEED A HUT!

BANG! THUD!

GOTCHA, WALTER!

YOU UTTER BARBARIAN, DENNIS!

SPLOTCH!

THERE'S OUR ROOF!

MUST BUILD SOMETHING TO TELL US THE TIME!

SHATTER! SMASH!

DAD'S ROCKERY.

A BRONZE AGE BOAR! BRILLIANT!

LEAP!

BRONZE AGE LIFE IS GREAT!

BUT IT'S DINNER TIME, PETS!

RUMBLE!

DAD WON'T NOTICE THE LITTLE GAP IN HIS FENCE!

NOW WE NEED SOME MUD FOR OUR HUT!

SLOSH!

THAT'LL SEAL UP THE DRAUGHTY BITS!

SPLOT! SPLUDGE!

WHO'S MAKING THAT RACKET AT TEN O' CLOCK IN THE MORNING?

SEE! OUR STONEHENGE CAN TELL US THE TIME!

WHERE'S RASHER OFF TO?

THARRUMPH! THARRUMPH!

GET OUT OF MY BARBER'S SHOP!

HAIRDRESSING PRICES.

ROLL!

CAN WE COME BACK TO THE PRESENT DAY, MUM?

ONE AGE TO GO THROUGH FIRST!

THE IRON AGE!

HUH!

I SUPPOSE MODERN BRITAIN'S NOT TOO BAD AFTER ALL!

HOME AND AWAY.

GNASHER

The Story of the Land

IF YOU LOOK on a map, you will probably recognize Britain. But millions of years ago the shape of Britain was very different. The continents have moved, changing the shape of the land. Britain's climate, rocks, and wildlife have changed as well.

THE MAKING OF AN ISLAND

Britain was not always an island. Until about 8,000 years ago, it was joined to Europe by a strip of land. Then, at the end of the last Ice Age, this strip of land was flooded.

FROZEN BRITAIN

Throughout history, there have been four main Ice Ages. In each Ice Age the Polar ice sheets expanded, covering much of the world in thick ice. During an Ice Age about 200,000BC many people left Britain. The north of England was completely covered in ice. Some people decided to stay but they had to learn to live in a colder, harsher Britain.

BRITAIN TODAY

Britain's mild wet climate makes much of the land green and fertile. In the south and east of England grain, fruit and vegetables are grown. Britain's main crops are barley, potatoes, wheat, and other vegetables. Dairy cows graze on pastures in western England and northern Ireland, while sheep feed on the uplands of Scotland and Wales. The highly populated southeast contains rolling chalk hills.

Early Peoples

PEOPLE FIRST lived in Europe as long ago as 250,000BC. Although there aren't written records of this time, we know how these people lived because of the evidence that has survived. These early people are called the people of the Old Stone Age. They were about 1.5 metres tall and survived by hunting wild animals and gathering nuts and fruit. They moved from place to place in groups and did not grow crops or domesticate animals.

CLUES TO THE PAST

People of the Old Stone Age used stone flake tools and hand-axes to hunt with. Sharp, flat pieces of flint were used to scrape skins and meat and flints with pointed ends were used to bore holes. As they became more skilled, they made hand-axes from blocks of stone.

2,000,000 years ago

500,000 years ago

250,000 years ago

10,000 years ago

6,000 years ago

Humans evolved over millions of years. The earliest people lived in Africa, but gradually moved throughout the world.

▲ The early Stone Age people were gifted artists. In France and Spain detailed paintings of hunting scenes have been discovered inside the caves they once inhabited. Cave artists used paint made of egg yolk and powdered minerals to record their daily lives.

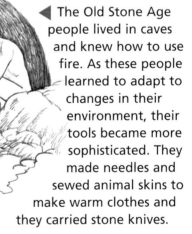

◄ The Old Stone Age people lived in caves and knew how to use fire. As these people learned to adapt to changes in their environment, their tools became more sophisticated. They made needles and sewed animal skins to make warm clothes and they carried stone knives.

UH-OH! IT'S A SABRE-TOOTHED ABYSSINIAN TRIPE HOUND!

DENNIS! BEHIND YOU!

IT'S TOO EARLY TO KEEP PETS!

AW! COME BACK IN A HUNDRED YEARS, PAL!

THE FIRST FARMERS

For thousands of years, people had been hunters and gatherers moving from place to place. One of the most far-reaching changes to occur was when people started to settle in one place and started farming the land. Planting crops and keeping animals had begun in the Middle East in about 7000BC. The first farmers appeared in Britain in 3500BC. They came from France bringing seed-corn, sheep and cattle. They lived in huts and established small settlements or villages. They buried their dead in long burial mounds.

FARMING METHODS

The early farmers are known as the people of the New Stone Age. They farmed using wooden ploughs. They harvested crops of wheat and barley using sickles made of flint. They used the shoulder-blades of cattle as shovels. As well as cattle and sheep, they kept pigs, goats and dogs.

▼ By the time of the last Ice Age, around 40,000 years BC, people living in Britain hunted with bows and arrows and ivory-tipped spears. They dressed in animal skins and wore head-dresses made from antlers to bring them luck when hunting. Let's hope that Minnie the Minx is lucky too! Their razor-sharp flint tools now had bone handles. By 10,000BC, when the climate had warmed up again, settlers from Europe brought with them strong tools to clear forests and make boats from felled trees.

FLINT MINING

Flint was used for so many things that people started mining it. This meant that large numbers of flint tools could be produced. Flint was also traded between other countries such as Ireland and France in exchange for seed and animals. A Stone Age flint mine was found at Grimes Graves in Norfolk. The mine reveals how the workers dug out the flint using bone tools.

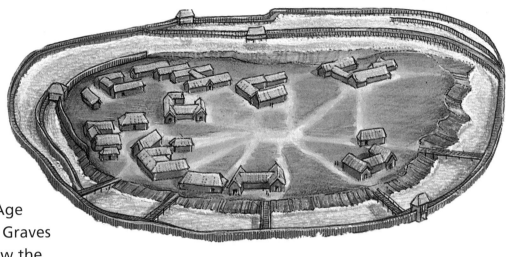

▲ Early settlements were made up of clusters of huts protected from invaders or wild animals by wooden fencing and ditches.

▼ One of the most fascinating early settlements was discovered at Skara Brae, in the Orkney Islands. It was built about 2000BC. There are a series of one-roomed stone huts linked by covered passages. As the landscape was harsh and windswept, there was very little wood, so even the furniture was made from stone.

THE BRONZE AGE

The knowledge of how to work with copper and bronze was brought to Britain by the Beaker people. They are called this because of the shape of the pottery mugs they made. Originally from Spain, they taught metal-

working to the people of Britain and Ireland about 3,500 years ago. Mining for metal was done by hand (above). Bronze farming tools and pots were made and traded throughout Europe. Bronze was also used to make luxury items such as musical instruments like these trumpets from Scandinavia (left) which produced a range of notes.

FARMING'S GREAT!

THEY'RE READY, NOW.

YOU CAN GROW PEAS FOR YOUR OWN PEA-SHOOTER!

The Celts

IN ABOUT 600BC, iron-using tribes settled in southern England. These new settlers came from Europe and were known as Celts. The ability to produce iron was a significant step forward in Britain. Iron is stronger than bronze and therefore better for making weapons and tools such as saws and axes.

CELTIC CRAFTS

The Celts were great artists and craftsmen and they produced beautiful bronze and iron jewellery, set with precious stones.

THE FIRST TOWNS

The Celts built great hill forts. Perhaps the best known is Maiden Castle in Dorset. Celtic settlements were the first towns in Britain. They built shops, workshops, temples and streets in and around the forts.

CELTIC TRADE

Around 1500BC, trade thrived between Britain and Gaul (France). Britons exported copper, bronze, tin and gold, woollen cloaks corn, dogs and slaves. They imported wine and pottery.

BOUDICCA
One of the most famous Celtic chiefs was Boudicca. When the Romans invaded Britain, Boudicca fought to protect her land. She led her people into battle, but killed herself when she realised they had no hope of winning.

▼ The Celts came from Turkey to Ireland. They settled in Britain and their descendants were known as Britons. They were expert horsemen and fierce warriors, as well as skilled farmers and surgeons.

55BC–AD407
The Romans in Britain
TIME CHART

All early dates are approximate. * denotes events that occurred outside Britain and Ireland.

55-54BC Julius Caesar makes raids on southern Britain.

7BC Cunobelinus is king of Catuvellauni, with capital at Colchester.

5BC *Jesus Christ is born.

AD30 *Jesus Christ is crucified.

43 Cunobelinus dies. Romans under Aulus Plautius invade England. Romans occupy Colchester. Romans begin the occupation of England. Roads and towns begin to be built.

48 Romans begin to occupy Wales.

60 First Roman villas are built.

61 Queen Boudicca leads revolt of Iceni. London is burnt. Boudicca dies. New London is started. Romans conquer Anglesey in Wales.

70 *Jerusalem is destroyed. Jews are exiled from Israel.

75 King Cogidubnus builds palace at Fishbourne, Sussex.

77-83 Julius Agricola is governor of Britain.

100 Roman villa is built at Lullingstone, Kent.

119 Caledonian clans in Scotland revolt, wiping out Roman Ninth Legion.

123 Hadrian's Wall is begun.

142 Antonine Wall in Scotland is started.

163 Romans retreat from Scotland to Hadrian's Wall.

196 Romans evacuate Hadrian's Wall. Scottish tribes capture York.

208 Romans occupy northern Britain and rebuild Hadrian's Wall.

270 *Roman Empire is collapsing.

280 First Saxon raiders attack southern England. Saxon Shore forts are built.

287 Albanus (later St Alban) becomes first Christian martyr in Britain.

296 Britain becomes part of Roman Empire again. Emperor Constantius invades Scotland.

306 Constantius dies at York; is succeeded by his son Constantine.

324 *Christianity becomes official religion of Roman Empire.

367 Roman control over Britain collapsing. Picts and Scots reach London. Roman general Theodosius restores Roman power.

388 Roman troops abandon Hadrian's Wall.

396 Picts invade northern Britain.

400 Romans begin to withdraw from Britain.

407 Last Roman troops leave Britain.

410 *Barbarian tribes sack Rome.

The Roman Invasions

BY THE LAST century BC, when Celtic tribes ruled Britain and Ireland, the Roman Empire stretched as far as the English Channel. The Romans hadn't actually conquered Britain but had traded peacefully for some time. But one Roman commander, Julius Caesar, was determined to invade Britain because he wanted to expand the Roman Empire.

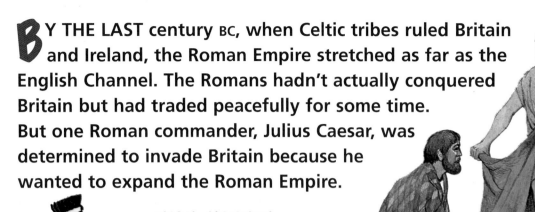

◀ British traders frequently travelled to Rome to sell woollen cloaks in the markets. A trader would risk attack from robbers on land and pirates at sea on his journey to buy and sell goods in Europe. Roman traders came to Britain with olive oil, wine and pottery which they traded for tin, iron ore, corn and gold and slaves. They discovered how rich the Celtic lands were, and decided to invade to extend the Roman Empire.

THE FIRST ROMAN ATTACK

Julius Caesar's first invasion in 55BC was a victory of sorts. After fierce fighting, the British, unsure of whether they could defeat these heavily armed invaders, asked for peace. However, the Romans had lost so many of their ships in the unpredictable British waters that Caesar decided to return to France.

CAESAR'S SECOND ATTACK

One year later, in 54BC, the Romans were back. This time they advanced as far as Canterbury. Rival tribes, who often

JULIUS CAESAR

Julius Caesar was a great Roman politician and military leader. He conquered many new territories for Rome, extending the Roman Empire into Gaul (France) and Germany. He took the title of dictator (sole ruler) for life in Rome but in 44BC, he was murdered by two of his senators, Brutus and Cassius, who thought that Caesar's ambitions would make him abolish the republic and declare himself king.

▼ The first Roman invasion took place at Deal on the Kent coast. The Romans found it very difficult to get ashore, and when they did they faced determined fighters ready to protect their country.

fought each other, united under one chief, Cassivellaunus, the leader of the Catuvellauni tribe from Colchester. When the Romans captured his headquarters, the British surrendered and accepted the Romans as overlords.

KING FOR A TIME

Although he was victorious, Caesar did not stay long in Britain. He returned to Rome a hero, where he eventually became the head of the Roman state.

▲ When attacking a Celtic stronghold, the Romans would advance on the main gate under cover of their shields. This was called a *testudo* or 'tortoise'.

▼ Roman soldiers were fully trained in military and defence tactics. Each soldier carried a shield, light armour, a spear and a short stabbing sword. Full-time soldiers had to be able to read and write.

THE ROMAN EMPIRE
The Romans left Britain alone for 90 years, not returning until AD43. This map shows the size of the Roman Empire (orange) before they invaded Britain. The Roman Army had reached the coast opposite Britain and was advancing into the Netherlands and Germany. It had already invaded Turkey, Spain and Portugal.

ROMAN RULE

It was not possible for the Romans to continually govern by force, so they involved the Britons in the daily running of the country as much as they could. British chiefs were made full Roman citizens and governed alongside the Romans. Local people joined the army, became magistrates and served on local councils. New farming and building methods were introduced by the Romans. Britons were encouraged to wear Roman clothes and adopt Roman customs and beliefs. But British civilians were not allowed to carry weapons and only Roman officials could collect taxes.

▲ Most Roman towns had public baths which contained a very hot steam room, a warm pool and a freezing cold pool. People would bathe, rest and relax.

▲ The Romans built many straight, wide roads. These new roads allowed the Roman army to march from place to place more quickly and made travelling to market with cartloads of produce easier.

▼ This medium-sized Roman villa would produce olive oil and grain which was stored in sunken jars in the courtyard. Vines were grown for wine and the kitchen garden supplied fresh fruit and vegetables.

400-1042
Invaders and Settlers
TIME CHART

*events that occurred outside Britain and Ireland.

By 400	*Anglo-Saxon mercenaries had begun to settle in Europe.
400-450	Saxons start permanent settlements in England.
432	St Patrick starts mission to Ireland.
450	Vortigern, the Welsh king, invites Saxons to settle in Thanet, Kent. Jutes accept.
457	Jutes defeat Britons at Crayford, Kent, and conquer all of Kent.
476	*Goths conquer Rome. End of western Roman Empire.
About 500	King Arthur leads Britons to victory over Saxons at Mount Badon, Dorset. Saxons settle most of southern England.
527	*Justinian Emperor of eastern Roman Empire (Byzantine).
563	St Columba founds Iona community.
570	*Muhammad is born.
588	Aethelric creates kingdom of Northumbria.
597	St Augustine starts mission to England.
600	England divided into seven Saxon kingdoms.
About 620	Sutton Hoo burial mound built.
632	*Muhammad dies.
635	Lindisfarne monastery is established.
About 650	Poem *Beowulf* is written.
664	Synod of Whitby formed.
732	*Muslim invasion of Europe halted at Battle of Tours.
757	Offa becomes King of Mercia.
774	Offa becomes Bretwalda (supreme ruler) of all England.
780	Norwegian tribes settle in Orkneys, Shetlands and Isle of Man.
787	First Viking raid on England.
By 800	Wales is divided into four main kingdoms.
800	*Charlemagne is crowned Emperor of western Europe.
835	Norwegians capture Dublin.
865	Danish Grand Army lands in eastern England.
866	York becomes the centre of a Norwegian empire.
871	Alfred is king of Wessex.
878	Alfred defeats Danes near Chippenham. Treaty of Wedmore divides England between Saxons and Danelaw.
899	King Alfred dies.
911	*Viking settlement is formed in Normandy.
924-975	King Athelstan and Edgar of Wessex unite most of England in peace.
959	St Dunstan is Archbishop of Canterbury.
980	Danes renew raids on England.
976-1016	Ethelred is king of Wessex.
1016	Danish King Canute is elected 'King of all England'.
1035	Canute dies. Seven years of fighting for succession follows.

Invaders and Settlers

THE ROMAN EMPIRE was vast, successful and progressive. But something so widespread was very difficult to control and govern. Much of the 3rd century of the Roman Empire was troubled and unruly. There were many threats of invasion from northern European tribes and civil wars broke out in many different regions of the Empire. Roman rule in Britain was also threatened by outsiders. Saxon tribes from Germany began to attack British shores. As Roger found out, the Romans built walls around their towns to protect them. For about 200 years, the Roman Empire struggled to survive. But by the 5th century, the Romans had left Britain for good, leaving the Saxons, Angles and other northern European tribes to take over Britain.

▲ Some of the invaders from Europe, especially those from Germany, were skilled metal-workers. They made weapons, helmets and armour, such as breastplates, of bronze, iron and silver.

▲ Saxon families landed in England and brought with them all their possessions including their farm animals.

ANGLES, SAXONS AND JUTES

From about AD450 tribes from northern Europe came to Britain in large numbers. Some were driven out of their lands in Germany, Scandinavia and the Netherlands by the Huns and the Goths, others were adventurers. By AD600, the invaders controlled most of England. The British were forced into northwest England, Cornwall, Devon and Wales. Those who did not leave worked as labourers or slaves on what was now Saxon land.

◄ The orange areas show where the Angles, Saxons and Jutes settled. The Angles went to what became Mercia, Deira Bernicia, east Anglia and Northumbria. The Jutes went to Kent. Wessex, Essex and Sussex became Saxon settlements.

▲ This Saxon helmet was made from iron, bronze and silver. It dates from about AD625.

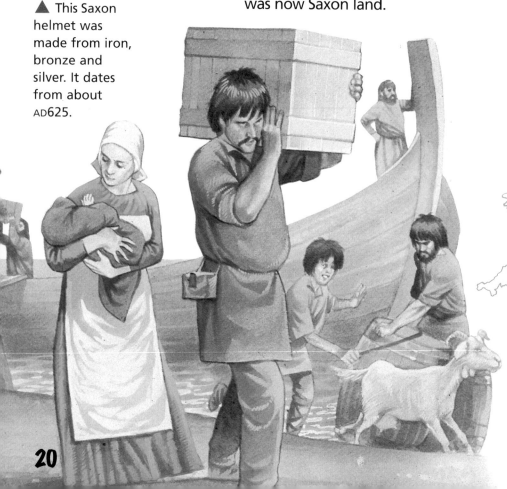

◄ The Saxons brought with them a way of life that was similar to life in Britain before the Romans invaded. The Saxons were farmers who lived in small settlements of about 50 people. They grew crops and kept sheep, cattle and goats. Loyalty to the family and tribe was the basis of Saxon life.

Picts and Celts

MANY BRITONS fled to Wales following the Anglo-Saxon invasion and settled into the local communities. In the 7th century, Scotland was inhabited by four different peoples. In the north and northeast lived the Picts. The tribes on the west coast were the Scots who were originally from Ireland and who gave their name to Scotland. In the Lowlands were the British tribes who had lived there since Roman times.

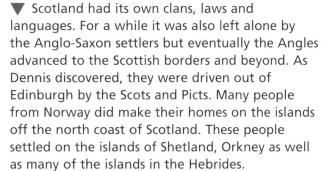

▲ For some time after the Anglo-Saxon tribes arrived in Britain the Welsh people were left alone by the Saxons. Many Britons had fled to Wales and had settled into Welsh society. Wales had previously consisted of many tiny kingdoms but by AD800 there were four main ones – Powys, Dyfed, Gwent and Gwynedd. Wales had its own unique culture, language and laws. The people lived in small villages in beehive-shaped huts with thatched roofs and low walls.

▼ Scotland had its own clans, laws and languages. For a while it was also left alone by the Anglo-Saxon settlers but eventually the Angles advanced to the Scottish borders and beyond. As Dennis discovered, they were driven out of Edinburgh by the Scots and Picts. Many people from Norway did make their homes on the islands off the north coast of Scotland. These people settled on the islands of Shetland, Orkney as well as many of the islands in the Hebrides.

IRELAND
The Anglo-Saxons did not conquer Ireland and Irish culture remained Celtic. At the time of the Anglo-Saxon invasion of Britain, most people in Ireland were still descendants of the Celtic tribes who had settled there in 300BC. Ireland consisted of five kingdoms, Ulster, Munster, Leinster, Meath and Connaught. Each kingdom was governed by a king.

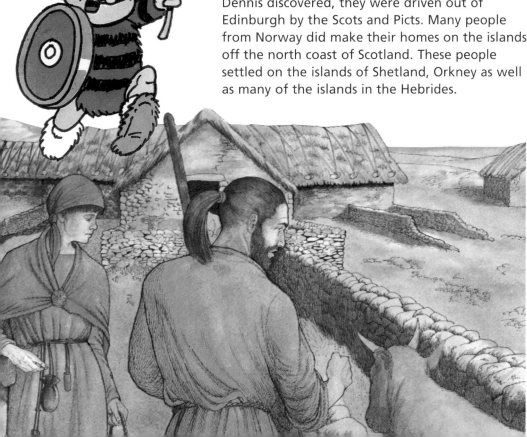

The Vikings

THE PATTERN of invading Britain continued. The Saxons, having displaced the Romans found themselves under threat of invasion in the 8th century when 'the men from the north' began to raid the northern coast of England. For these men from Norway and Denmark were in search of new lands and saw Britain as an ideal place to settle, so Teacher had better watch out! In Norway, land was scarce and the population was growing. By AD865, the Danish Grand Army had landed on the east coast of England with the intention of invading. Five years later, Wessex, the most important English kingdom, was about to fall.

▲ The sight of a Viking longboat terrified the people of Britain. The Vikings seized land, burnt villages and raided monasteries.

▶ The Vikings were skilled metal-workers. They also made gold and silver jewellery and swords and axes from iron.

ALFRED THE GREAT

Rather than face defeat, Alfred the Great, king of Wessex, paid the Danes to leave his kingdom alone. He bought just five years of peace. In that time the Danes conquered Mercia and went on to take over one-third of England. Then they returned to take Wessex. Alfred fought and defeated the Danes and their leader, King Guthrum, asked for peace. The Danish settled peacefully, and gradually England became united. Canute, a Dane, was crowned King of all England in 1016.

▶ The Vikings settled in an area of Britain which became known as Danelaw.

Danelaw

English Mercia

Wessex

VIKING GODS
The Vikings worshipped many different gods, but there were three that were especially important. Odin, the leader of the gods, was the god of knowledge and war. Thor, provided protection from cold, hunger, giants and other dangers. Frey was the goddess of love and beauty.

The Norman Conquest

AFTER KING CANUTE died there followed a great deal of unrest about who should become King of England. Finally, in 1042, Edward, Alfred's great-great-great-grandson, became king. His reputation as a devout Christian earned him the name 'the Confessor', meaning 'strong believer in the faith'. During Edward's reign, England became the strongest kingdom in Europe.

But, when Edward died without an heir in 1066, four men claimed the throne. They were, William, Duke of Normandy, Harold Hardrada from Norway, Harold of Wessex and Tostig, Earl of Northumbria.

THE NEW KING

Before he died, Edward chose Harold of Wessex to follow him as king. Harold was crowned but not everyone agreed that he should be king. Harold's strongest challenge came from William, Duke of Normandy.

THE BATTLE OF HASTINGS

On September 28, 1066, William, Duke of Normandy, landed on the Sussex coast near Hastings. On October 14, 1066, the battle of Hastings began. By nightfall the English were defeated and Harold was dead. William then set off for London. He met some resistance on the way but in the end he was victorious. He was crowned King of England in Westminster Abbey on Christmas Day, 1066.

A motte and bailey castle

Castle with stone stronghold

THE DOMESDAY BOOK

William wanted to know how much land there was in his new kingdom and how much it was worth. He also wanted to work out how much tax his landowners should pay. So, in 1084, he commissioned a survey. It took two years to complete and covered all of England except London and Winchester and some parts of the far north. The survey revealed that the English population was about one million and that 90 per cent worked on the land.

BRITAIN UNDER THE NORMANS

For many years there was much resistance to William. He ruled with brutal force and severely punished any rebels. His opponents were not just the local people. Others, such as the Danes and the Scots, also attacked him. He burnt towns and villages and starved the people who lived in them. He invaded Scotland and the lowland areas of south Wales. The Normans found it difficult to advance further into Wales because of the mountain ranges.

CASTLES AND FORTS

To defend their newly conquered lands the Normans built many castles and forts, the most famous being the Tower of London. England and northern France were now one nation with one king. William was succeeded by his sons, William II and Henry I, and as a result of increased trade, England became wealthier than ever before.

Stone castle with towers

Castle with outer walls

Early castles were made of wood and built on a motte or mound. Some had moats. Later castles were made of stone and had high towers and thick outer walls.

◀ In Norman England the people enjoyed telling romantic stories of love, honour and chivalry between knights and ladies of the royal court. These stories are known as 'courtly love'.

The Feudal System

WILLIAM THE CONQUEROR introduced a system in England which divided society so that everyone knew their roles and position. The king was the supreme ruler. He kept much of the land for himself, stopping people from entering or hunting in the royal forests or woodlands. The king relied upon his barons, earls and church leaders to help him govern. Knights answered to the barons and earls and were employed by them to fight the king's battles.

▲ Pigs were kept for their meat.

FARMING

People who worked on the land did so from first light until darkness. Winter weather sometimes made it difficult to work, especially if the ground was frozen. Ploughing and sowing took place in spring and haymaking began in June. Crops were harvested in August and animals were slaughtered before winter as they could not be fed during this time. The meat was eaten or preserved in salt. Women and children were expected to work in the fields all year round.

▲ Sickles or scythes like this were used to cut the corn at harvest time.

VILLEINS AND SERFS

The largest group of the population in Norman England were 'villeins' who leased land for farming and also worked on the landlord's land. Below them were the serfs who had no rights and were basically slaves.

▼Villeins lived in houses made of wattle and daub. Roofs were thatched and houses did not have windows.

27

The Middle Ages

THE MIDDLE AGES, or the Medieval era, fall between what we call ancient and modern times. This period covers almost 300 years of history and during this time there were many changes in Britain. By now an average town contained about 5,000 people although most people still lived in the countryside. Those living in towns were employed in trading or manufacturing. It was unusual to have more than two children, so Sidney and Toots would have been okay. Most people could not read or write. The Church was very powerful and controlled people's lives. Every village had its own church and almost everyone attended on Sundays and holy days.

▲ The Great Seal of King John (1199-1216) was used to seal the Magna Carta. John was a very unpopular king. In 1214 the English barons revolted against him and forced him to make changes to the way he governed. They listed their demands in a charter known as the Magna Carta, or great charter. The charter demanded that people could not be punished without a trial and that taxes could not be raised without the barons' agreement. These new laws applied only to the rich and powerful and most people's rights stayed the same.

▼ The beginning of the Middle Ages were dominated by the Crusades or 'wars of the cross'. European Christians went on campaigns to the Holy Lands, including Jerusalem, to free them from the occupation of the Turkish Muslims.

MEDIEVAL KINGS

After the death of William the Conqueror and his sons, there once again followed years of fighting over who should be the king of England. This was finally settled when William the Conqueror's great-grandson, Henry II, was crowned. When Henry II died, he was succeeded by Richard I, or Richard the Lionheart as he was known. Richard spent many years fighting in the Crusades, or holy wars. He was succeeded by his brother John after he died fighting in France.

WARS OF THE ROSES

Once again, who should have the throne of England became the cause of bitter fighting. From 1455, a series of civil wars were fought between the followers of two houses, York and Lancaster, both of whom claimed the throne. Henry VI represented the red rose of the House of Lancaster and Richard, Duke of York, who had been acting as protector of the realm during Henry VI's illness, the white rose of the House of York. These wars were known as the Wars of the Roses. In 1461 Richard's son Edward IV claimed the throne and ruled for 12 years.

▲ At this time, Scotland was a separate nation. It had its own coinage, customs and kings. The Scots did not welcome the English interfering with the way they ruled themselves. But for many years, English kings had tried to control Scotland. Many fierce battles were fought and lost by both sides. Eventually, in 1328, Scotland finally became independent and Robert Bruce was recognized as the first overall king of Scotland.

▲ Open sewers and unhygienic conditions meant that not many people lived to be older than 40. In 1349 the Black Death struck. The Black Death was an illness spread by fleas which were carried by black rats. There was no cure for it. One in three people in England died of the Black Death.

KEEP TRYING After two English defeats and eight years of war, Robert Bruce went into hiding. He watched a spider try seven times to climb up its web before reaching its goal. This inspired him to renew the battle which he won.

The Tudors

THE WARS of the Roses finally ended when Henry VII of the House of Lancaster married Elizabeth of York in 1486. Henry VII brought the government under control and increased the power of the throne. He also made peace with France and Scotland.

▲ In 1509 Henry VIII became king and also married his brother's widow, a Spanish princess called Catherine of Aragon. The marriage between them was against Church law because Catherine was Henry's brother's widow, but the Pope granted Henry special permission so that he could marry Catherine. This was to cause the monarchy problems later on.

HENRY AND THE POPE

In 1509 Henry VII died and, at the age of 17, Henry VIII became king. Henry was desperate for a son and although his wife Catherine had given birth to seven children, only one had survived, a daughter called Mary. So Henry wanted his marriage to be declared illegal by the Church. Only the Pope could do this and he refused. Henry had found a new love, Anne Boleyn, who was expecting his child. Henry was convinced it was going to be a boy. He decided to set up a new

▲ Henry VIII decided to close many of England's monasteries, gaining wealth by taking over their funds and selling off their land. If the monks resisted they were killed brutally. In just 10 years Henry closed all of England's 800 monasteries.

▼ King Philip II of Spain sent the Spanish Armada to invade England in August 1588. They were defeated before they even set foot on English soil.

William Shakespeare (1564-1616) was a playwright, poet, actor and theatre manager. He was involved with running the Globe Theatre at Southwark, in London. At this time the audience sat on the stage with the actors and cheered, booed or threw rubbish at the actors depending on how they enjoyed the performance.

church which would be separate from Rome, divorce Catherine and marry Anne. As a result of his divorce, the Pope excommunicated Henry from the Catholic Church. In September 1533, Anne gave birth to a girl, called Elizabeth. Still wanting a boy, Henry had to get rid of Anne so that he could remarry. He accused her of being unfaithful and she was beheaded.

HENRY'S OTHER WIVES

After Anne's death, Henry married Jane Seymour. Finally, with Jane, Henry had a son, called Edward. Sadly, Jane died soon after giving birth. Henry divorced his next wife, Anne of Cleves and beheaded his fifth wife, Katherine Howard. But his last wife, Catherine Parr, outlived him.

AFTER HENRY

Henry VIII's son, Edward VI, became king at the age of nine. He died in 1553 at the age of 16. Mary I then ruled until her death in 1558. This allowed Henry VIII and Anne Boleyn's daughter, Elizabeth, to become queen. Her reign was long and relatively peaceful.

ELIZABETH I
Elizabeth I became queen at the age of 25. She encouraged exploration, rewarding success with knighthoods and other honours. She successfully held her one true opponent, Mary, Queen of Scots, captive for 19 years.

QUEEN MIN'S GOING TO THE EXECUTIONER'S BLOCK!

THANKS! I WONDERED HOW I WAS GOING TO OPEN MY COCONUT!

The Stuarts

WHEN ELIZABETH died in 1603, the son of Mary, Queen of Scots, James VI of Scotland, became King James I of England. James had been king of Scotland since the age of two. He was 37 when he succeeded to the English throne and began the English Stuart line. James started his reign by ending the wars with Spain. They had been expensive and little had been achieved. His ambition was to unite England and Scotland.

TROUBLE WITH PARLIAMENT

Almost immediately James became an unpopular king. He appointed his own courtiers to high ranking positions and gave them land and power. His court was very extravagant and expensive, and James soon needed to raise money to pay for it. He believed that as the head of the Church, he had a divine right to rule. He tried to govern without consulting Parliament, and even raised taxes without their consent. Then, in 1625, James suddenly died.

GUY FAWKES

On November 5, 1605, a group of Roman Catholics including a man called Guy Fawkes, attempted to kill James I, by blowing up the Houses of Parliament. Their plot was discovered and they were tortured and executed as traitors.

▼ The slave trade was started by the Spanish and Portuguese in the 16th century. By the 17th century more than 100,000 slaves from Africa were being shipped to plantations in the southern states of America. Inside the ships the slaves were chained to each other.

CHARLES I

After the death of his father, Charles I was crowned in 1625. His marriage to the French Roman Catholic princess, Henrietta Maria, did not please his countrymen. And, like his father James I, Charles believed that kings should be able to do as they pleased. For more than 11 years he ruled without Parliament, raising taxes without consulting them. This period of government by Charles and a small group of ministers ended when Charles needed money to pay for an army to fight the Scottish Puritans and Presbyterians. Because Charles now needed Parliament, many MPs insisted that he agree to certain demands. At first he did, but when they demanded the right to appoint his council of ministers, he refused. A bloody civil war followed.

THE KING JAMES BIBLE

The King James Bible was produced under the supervision of James I. This version of the English bible was one of the most important books in England for hundreds of years. It was started in 1604. Fifty scholars worked on it over several years, and it was completed in 1611.

◄ In 1620 a group of Puritans left England on board a ship called *The Mayflower*, bound for America where they hoped to set up a new life, free from religious persecution. This group established a settlement in Massachusetts, in an area which became known as New England.

The Civil War

THE CIVIL WAR was fought to find out who would rule the country – the king or Parliament – and Plug wants to find out who to support. Landowners and Church leaders were loyal to the king. Most of Parliament's support came from London and many Puritans. Success depended upon who Scotland would support. The Parliamentarians had a strong army led by Oliver Cromwell and Sir Thomas Fairfax. In 1643, the Scots joined the fight on the side of Parliament.

▲ In 1644-1645, Cromwell formed an army called the New Model Army. Cromwell's supporters were known as 'Roundheads', because of their close-cut hair. The Royalists were called 'Cavaliers'.

THE COMMONWEALTH

England was now a country without a king – the government announced that it was a Commonwealth. Many countries, including France, Spain, Holland, Ireland and Scotland declared war on it, but all were defeated by Cromwell.

OLIVER CROMWELL

In 1653 Cromwell took the title of Lord Protector and ruled the country with the help of the army. He was ruthless with those who opposed him. In Ireland, he seized two-thirds of the land and gave it to English landowners. After Cromwell's death in 1658, his son Richard, tried to rule, but was unable to govern as well as his father. He resigned in 1659.

THE DEFEAT OF A KING

The Royalists were completely defeated by Cromwell's army at Naseby in 1645. But still Charles refused to surrender any of his power. Although he was in prison, Charles finally gained the support of the Scots and a second civil war broke out. Once again he was defeated. He was tried and found guilty of treason.

◄ On January 20, 1649 Charles I was found guilty of treason and was sentenced to death. The day of his execution, January 30, was bitterly cold, so Charles wore two shirts. He didn't want to shiver and have people think that he was afraid. He was beheaded outside Whitehall Palace, in London.

CHARLES II

In May of 1660, Charles I's son, having fled to Europe as a child, returned to England. Charles II agreed to share power with Parliament and to be tolerant of religious beliefs. He also agreed that Parliament could not be dismissed without its own consent and that taxes had to be raised through Parliament. Charles was happy to agree and did not seek revenge for his father's death, but the new Parliament did. It sought the deaths of all those who had signed Charles I's death warrant.

CHARLES II AND PARLIAMENT

The truce between Parliament and the king did not last long. By 1672, Charles had dismissed Parliament and was trying to overturn laws which had been passed against Roman Catholics. But he backed down as the opposition was too strong.

A RIGHTFUL HEIR

Rumours, mostly unfounded, linked the king's brother, James, with plots to overthrow the king, return Britain to Catholicism and seize the throne. James was in fact the heir to the throne as his brother the king, did not

◀ William and Mary were declared joint rulers in 1689. They ruled with Parliament. In 1689, they passed The Bill of Rights stating that a Catholic could not become king or queen of Britain.

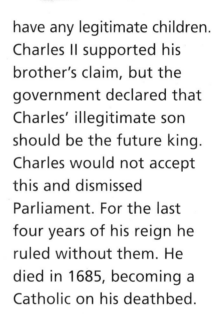

have any legitimate children. Charles II supported his brother's claim, but the government declared that Charles' illegitimate son should be the future king. Charles would not accept this and dismissed Parliament. For the last four years of his reign he ruled without them. He died in 1685, becoming a Catholic on his deathbed.

JAMES II

Charles II's wish was granted. James II came to the throne after Charles' death. His reign was brief however. Parliament now wanted James' daughter Mary, and her Protestant husband William, to take the throne. They were so determined that they invited William and Mary to invade Britain 'secretly'. They did so in 1688, and James fled to France.

▲ In the mid-1660s two disasters struck London. In 1665 the Great Plague killed about 70,000 people. The bodies of the dead were loaded on to carts and buried outside the city. In 1666 the Great Fire started. Over 100,000 people were made homeless but it did help to rid the city of the plague.

SOPPY LITTLE GIRLIE!

WE'RE HAVING AN UNCIVIL WAR!

18th Century Britain

THE 18TH CENTURY began with an historic act. The Act of Union of 1707 joined England and Scotland to form a "United Kingdom". In 1714, George I, the Protestant ruler of a German state and great-grandson of James I, succeeded to the British throne. Many Scots resisted this. Their chosen ruler was James II's Catholic son, James Edward Stuart. His supporters were called Jacobites.

OFF TO WAR

George II came to the throne in 1727. By the middle of the century, Britain was fighting France in Europe (The Seven Years War). But it was to be wars over colonies in the West Indies, India and Canada that proved to be the most challenging of all.

THE JACOBITES

In 1745, James Edward Stuart's son Charles ("Bonnie Prince Charlie"), led the Jacobites in a strong attack against the English. The Jacobites were eventually defeated by the English at Culloden. Charles left Britain, and died in 1788. To punish the Jacobites for their rebellion, the English, helped by Scottish landlords, cleared the Highlands by burning villages and turning tenant farmers off their land. The landlords saw this as a way to modernize their farming methods.

▼ America was a valuable British colony, but it wanted more freedom to determine its future. After a protest about unfair taxes in Boston, 13 states declared themselves independent of Britain and war began. After seven years of fighting, the British Army surrendered in 1781 and independence was granted in 1783.

▲ The Scottish Jacobite rebellion of 1745 was finally crushed by the English army at the battle of Culloden (1746). The battle was over in about 40 minutes. To punish the Jacobites, the English burned villages and banned the clans from wearing tartan and playing bagpipes.

THE ACT OF UNION
This Act united England and Scotland. The English flag and the Scottish flag were joined to make the Union Flag.

With increased industry in the towns, people had to find a way to get raw materials to the factories cheaply. Canals were built so that barges could carry heavy goods such as coal easily. By 1800 there was a network of canals across the country. Many people travelled by stagecoach, although road conditions were bad and travellers were at risk from highwaymen.

NEW INVENTIONS
In the 18th century, there was a new interest in farming. New crops were grown, better animals were bred and new farming methods were introduced.

THE INDUSTRIAL REVOLUTION

In 1801, there were about 10 million people in Britain. Over the next 50 years, Britain became the most advanced industrial power in the world. With the rapid development of factories, mills and mines, thousands of people left the land and flooded into towns – some new, some having to develop very quickly – all over Britain. People lived in cramped, unhygienic conditions. They worked 12 or 14 hours a day just to survive.

THE LUDDITES

The livelihoods of those who did not seek work in the towns were threatened by the new factories. Some people, following a man called Ned Ludd, smashed factory machinery. They were known as Luddites.

▲ Children aged six and over were employed in factories or mines to carry out what were considered simple tasks. In 1833, the Factory Act was passed which prevented children under nine working in textile mills. Children aged nine to thirteen could not work longer than 12 hours. Inspectors were appointed to make sure this happened.

The Victorians

WILLIAM IV died in 1837. He had become king following the death of his brother George IV. William had died childless and so his niece, Victoria, became queen at the age of 18. She was to reign for 64 years. At the age of 21, Queen Victoria married Prince Albert, a German prince. They were happily married for 20 years until he died of typhoid in 1861. During Victoria's reign the British Empire was at its greatest, and in 1858, Victoria was crowned Empress of India. Her reign also saw some improvements in health care, advances in education and transport as Ivy discovered, and more people had the right to vote in Parliamentary elections.

▲ In Victorian Britain, if poor people needed help, they had to leave their homes and enter workhouses. Husbands, wives and children were separated from each other. They all had to work long hours and were given little to eat.

SLAVE TRADE ABOLISHED

Since the 16th century, the slave trade had made people very rich. One man, William Wilberforce, campaigned against it for most of his life. He showed Parliament evidence of the incredible cruelty suffered by slaves. In 1807 British ships were banned from trading in slaves, and finally, in 1833, slavery was made illegal in all parts of the British Empire.

THE CHARTISTS

Quiet mumblings of 'one man, one vote', and improved conditions for the working classes grew in the 19th century into public protest. One group drew up a charter in which they demanded that all men should have the right to vote and that votes should be secret. They also wanted anyone to be able to become an MP regardless of their background. This group of men were known as Chartists. They did not succeed in achieving their aims then, but almost all of their demands are part of British law today.

POSTING LETTERS

Until 1840, the receiver of a letter paid for its delivery. With the development of the railway came the penny post. A penny was the charge per half ounce to anywhere in the Empire.

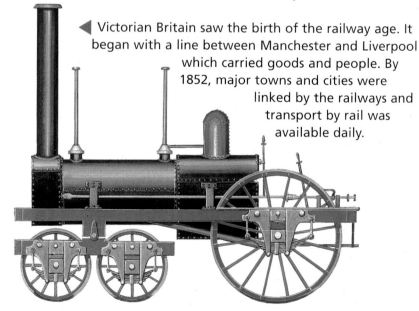

◀ Victorian Britain saw the birth of the railway age. It began with a line between Manchester and Liverpool which carried goods and people. By 1852, major towns and cities were linked by the railways and transport by rail was available daily.

ISAMBARD KINGDOM BRUNEL

Brunel was a great Victorian engineer and inventor. He designed the Great Western Railway which joined London to Bristol. He also designed three famous steamships: the *Great Western*, the first steamship to cross the Atlantic, the *Great Britain*, the first ocean steamship with a screw propeller and the *Great Eastern*, which was, until 1899, the largest vessel ever built. In 1829-1831 Brunel designed the Clifton Suspension Bridge in Bristol. It was completed in 1864. The road is suspended on cables.

Between 1800 and 1845, the population in Ireland doubled to 8,500,000. At least half were poor people who relied on potatoes as their main source of food and income. In 1845, and again in 1846, about three-quarters of the potato crop was destroyed by a disease called blight. As a result, many people could not pay their rents and so were turned out of their homes. Following the potato blight in Ireland nearly 1,000,000 people died of hunger and thousands emigrated to Britain, Australia and North America. Between 1845 and 1851 the Irish population fell by nearly 25 per cent.

HEALTH CARE

Towns were filthy and dangerous. In 1851, if you lived in Manchester or Liverpool, you would have been lucky to live past the age of 25 years. Typhoid and cholera spread through the overcrowded houses and streets. There was no fresh running water and sewage was dumped in the streets or nearby rivers. Edwin Chadwick's Public Health Act of 1848 set up a Board of Health in London to improve conditions.

The Twentieth Century

QUEEN VICTORIA died in 1901 aged 82. It was the end of an era. In 1901 Edward VII became king. His reign was short and in 1910 George V came to the throne. In the 20th century the world was to change dramatically. Two world wars were fought with millions of people dying. In Britain, women eventually got the vote and the Irish Republic was formed. The Empire was no more and, after spending centuries fighting wars in Europe, Britain joined the European Union.

THE SUFFRAGETTES

In 1903, Emmeline Pankhurst formed the Women's Social and Political Union. Their aim was to achieve the vote for women. They began by speaking in public, writing letters and signing petitions. But when this failed to achieve the desired response, they became more militant. They chained themselves to railings, smashed windows, and held protest marches and rallies. Many were imprisoned. When World War I began, they still did not have the vote. But their work during the war helped their cause. In June 1918, a Bill was passed granting women aged 30 and over the right to vote.

BETWEEN THE WARS

Before World War I, the Labour Party was beginning to gain support. It was a party that worked closely with the Trade Unions and spoke out about the

▲ Aircraft, such as the German Fokker triplane (top left), were first used during World War I. Tanks, such as the British MK IV (bottom), were also used. Gas masks (top right) were issued to all soldiers.

▶ On August 4, 1914, Britain declared war on Germany. The Germans had attacked Belgium and were planning to invade France. More than 1,000,000 British men were killed and about 2,000,000 were injured in the war. Germany finally surrendered on November 11, 1918.

In the comic panels:
"I'VE JUST SEEN MINNIE WITH A TANK!"
"DIG TRENCHES! PUT UP BARRICADES!"
"NEW TANK FOR YOUR BIRTHDAY GOLDIE!"
"OOH! THOUGHT IT WAS AN ARMY TANK!"

IRELAND

In 1916, a group of men seized the Dublin General Post Office and proclaimed an Independent Ireland. These men were captured and shot by the British. When elections followed in 1918, the Irish general public expressed their disapproval for the treatment of these men by voting for their own representatives. The newly elected men set up an Irish Government, no longer recognizing Britain. This action brought about war between Britain and Ireland. It was a war that lasted for three years until, in 1921, Lloyd George signed a treaty with Ireland. Eighty per cent of Ireland became free of British rule. Ulster Unionists refused to allow Ulster to become part of a united Ireland, and so it has continued to be part of the United Kingdom.

need to improve the conditions of the poorest people in Britain. In 1923, the first Labour government was elected under Ramsay MacDonald. But it wasn't until after World War II that the Labour Party were able to introduce significant changes to the British way of life.

In the general election of 1945 the Labour Party, under their leader, Clement Attlee, swept to power. They introduced a welfare programme which included the introduction of National Insurance whereby everyone who worked had to pay some money into a national insurance fund. The National Health Service, launched in 1948, provided free health care.

▼ Between 1925 and 1926, miners were asked to accept lower wages and longer hours. They refused and went on strike. Many other unions went on strike in sympathy. This was known as the General Strike. For a while Britain came close to a complete shutdown. But the government would not give in and the miners had to return to work for lower wages.

WORLD WAR II

In 1933, Adolf Hitler became Chancellor of Germany. He was eager for revenge after Germany's defeat in 1918. The Germans invaded Czechoslovakia and Poland. These actions brought Britain into a devastating World War. By 1940, Germany had taken control of Denmark, Norway and Holland. The worst blow happened on June 22, 1940, when France surrendered. Until Russia and the USA entered the war in 1941, Britain had to fight alone.

During the war, Winston Churchill became Prime Minister. He was a strong leader and gave the British people hope.

THE BLITZ

For one month in 1940, between August and September, German aircraft bombed southeast England. Then from September to November, they bombed London every night. This was known as the Blitz.

The USA entered the war in 1941. In June 1944, British and American troops landed in Normandy in northern France. This was to turn the tide of war in favour of the Allies.

◀ In July 1940, Germany's air force, the Luftwaffe, began to bomb British cities. Hitler had ordered the destruction of the British air force (RAF) and the Battle of Britain began. The RAF destroyed 1,733 Luftwaffe planes. Although they lost 915 planes, the RAF won the Battle.

▼ In August 1945, the first atomic bombs were dropped by the USA on the Japanese cities of Hiroshima and Nagasaki. Over 200,000 people were killed and about the same number injured.

THE HOUSE OF WINDSOR

Edward VII (1901-1910). He was the eldest son of Queen Victoria and was nearly 60 when he came to the throne.

George V (1910-1936). His reign saw the outbreak of World War I and violent trouble in Ireland.

George VI (1936-1952) was Edward's younger brother, and never expected to be king.

Edward VIII (1936) was the eldest son of George V. He gave up the throne to marry an American divorcee, Mrs Wallis Simpson.

Queen Elizabeth II (1952-) is the eldest daughter of George VI and became queen at the age of 25.

Tall Tales

BRITAIN RESOUNDS with tales of honourable kings, magical wizards and evil-eyed witches. Myths and legends are not *just* stories told to entertain the listener. They are often stories with hidden meanings, which attempt to explain the inexplicable. Many myths and legends have survived for hundreds of years, because the stories are so captivating.

MYTH OR LEGEND?

Legends are stories that are told as if they are true, but which cannot be proved. They may involve the made-up adventures of a real person. Many ancient peoples believed in different gods and spirits. Stories about the gods are called myths. The study of myths is called mythology.

▼King Arthur is the legendary king of 6th century Britain. A legend tells of Arthur's childhood with the magician Merlin, how he fought the Anglo-Saxon invaders and how he was given a magical sword, called Excalibur, by the Lady of the Lake.

CU CHULAINN

Cu Chulainn was a legendary Irish hero who defended Ulster against the queen of Connacht. All the warriors of Ulster had been stricken with a sickness – all except Cu Chulainn and his father. The two men fought and won against the entire forces of Connacht.

Billy Whizz

TODAY I'M GOING TO RUN FROM LAND'S END TO JOHN O'GROATS!

SHORT-CUT TIME!

I'M OFF AGAIN!

BAH! FOG!

IF I RUN FAST I'LL BURN IT OFF.

OH, NO! I'VE RUN TO FRANCE!

HEY!

BAH! I'VE BEEN DELIVERED TO MY OWN STREET.

DON'T SEE ANY PROBLEMS THIS TIME.

SCHOOL

Around Britain

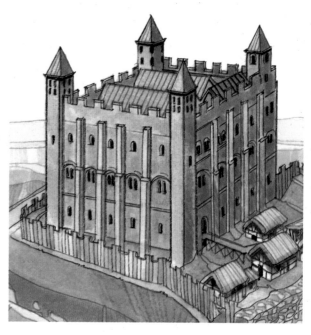

BRITAIN IS an island country and the surrounding sea gives Britain a varied climate. It has helped the mainland to resist invasion ever since the Normans arrived 900 years ago. Its rich history and changing landscape make Britain a fascinating place to explore. There are towering mountains, rolling hills and fields, windswept moors, cliffs and tranquil lakes. In contrast, there are bustling towns with huge shopping centres and sprawling road systems.

▶ There are beautiful old churches all over Britain. The first church of St Martin at Canterbury was built when the Romans occupied Britain. The church of St Laurence at Bradford-on-Avon in Wiltshire dates from Saxon times.

WHAT'S IN A NAME?

When people talk about the British Isles, they mean the United Kingdom and Ireland. The United Kingdom, also known as Britain, includes England, Wales, Scotland, Northern Ireland and the Channel Islands.

THE BRITISH PEOPLE

The British people are as varied as Britain itself. Throughout history, different peoples have settled here. The very first Britons walked across from mainland Europe before the English Channel became sea. More recently, many people from countries that were once part of the British Empire have made Britain their home.

▲ The Tower of London was built by the Normans in the 11th century. It has been a royal palace and a prison, as well as a place for torture and execution.

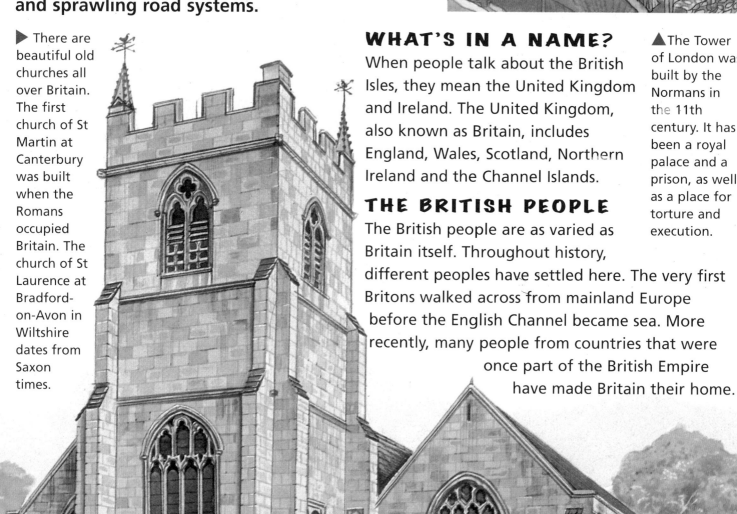

GETTING AROUND

There are thousands of kilometres of roads in Britain, with more being built every year.

M roads are motorways. Their direction and distance signs are blue. Because they are designed to be fast roads, learner drivers, cyclists, walkers and animals are not allowed on them.

A roads are the main routes between towns. Their direction and distance signs are green.

B roads are slower routes between villages. White signposts give directions and distances.

Railways have different kinds of routes. InterCity trains allow fast travel between major cities.

Britain needs good sea and air transport for international travel because it is surrounded by sea.

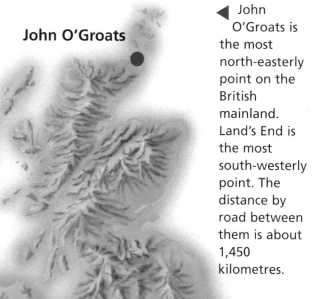

John O'Groats

Land's End

◄ John O'Groats is the most north-easterly point on the British mainland. Land's End is the most south-westerly point. The distance by road between them is about 1,450 kilometres.

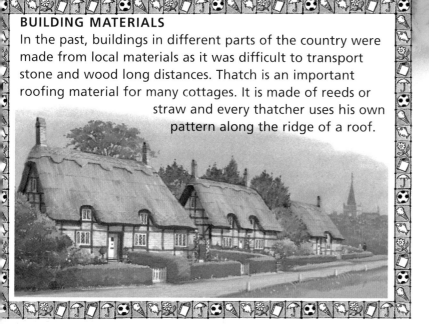

BUILDING MATERIALS

In the past, buildings in different parts of the country were made from local materials as it was difficult to transport stone and wood long distances. Thatch is an important roofing material for many cottages. It is made of reeds or straw and every thatcher uses his own pattern along the ridge of a roof.

Southern England

SOUTHERN ENGLAND contains some of Britain's best farmland, although there are rolling hills and ancient forests too. The capital of Britain, London, is the place of work for many people living in the city itself, or living in the surrounding suburbs, towns and countryside.

TREASURE TROVE

East Anglia, the part of England that bulges out into the North Sea, has a long history of being settled by different peoples. In recent years, several hordes of treasure have been found here, buried by the Romans or the tribes that came before them. The latest was found when a man was looking for a lost hammer!

▲ Stonehenge was built over 4,000 years ago and is one of the most famous prehistoric monuments in Europe.

London attracts about 23,000,000 visitors every year.

CANTERBURY

Canterbury is an historic city in Kent. It is famous for its beautiful cathedral built from the 11th to 15th centuries. The cathedral became a place of pilgrimage in the Middle Ages following the murder in 1170 of the then Archbishop of Canterbury, Thomas à Becket, on the altar steps.

▼ The New Forest in Hampshire is not new at all. It was once a royal hunting forest and is still a good place to ride. New Forest ponies roam freely there too. Britain was once covered by ancient forests, but now only a fraction of these native woodlands are left.

▼ Royal figures such as the Prince Regent (later George IV) made seaside resorts like Brighton fashionable. The Royal Pavilion was rebuilt for him to look like an Indian palace.

LONDON UNDERGROUND DOESN'T SEEM TO HAVE ANY TRAINS!

SO I'M NOT WAITING ANY LONGER!

▲ London has many famous historic buildings which attract thousands of tourists every year.

LONDON

The capital of Britain, London, was probably founded by the Romans. It is now home to over 7,000,000 people. The River Thames, running through the city, once brought large ships right into the heart of the capital. The oldest part of London is now the financial centre, and is called simply 'the City'.

OUT AND ABOUT

London was the first city in the world to have an underground railway, known as the 'Tube'. The first line was built in 1890. Double-decker buses and black taxis are a typical sight on the capital's busy roads, although it is said that because of the amount of traffic, they cannot move any faster than horsedrawn vehicles did at the beginning of the century!

◄ Guards stand in front of sentry boxes outside Buckingham Palace, guarding the Queen. When she is there, the Royal Standard is flown from the flagpole.

IMPORTANT BUILDINGS

Westminster Abbey has been the scene of the coronation of every British king and queen since 1066. St Paul's Cathedral was designed by Sir Christopher Wren. It replaced the one that burned down in the Fire of London in 1666. The best known part of the Houses of Parliament is Big Ben, which is the bell inside the clock tower, not the tower itself.

Cockneys are said to be Londoners born within hearing of the bells of Bow church.

The name of the city comes from Londinium, which is its Roman title.

▼ Many famous bridges span the Thames and a new one is planned to celebrate the millennium. The nursery rhyme "London Bridge is Falling Down" is based on an historical event. In 1014 Viking invaders attached ships to an early London Bridge and pulled it down.

49

Northern England

IT IS IN northern England that the iron ore and coal was found that made Britain the first great industrial nation. But as well as the large cities that grew up at this time, northern England has huge areas of unspoilt scenery, ideal for walkers and outdoor holidays.

SCENERY TO INSPIRE

Some of the most beautiful countryside in Britain is in the north. Much of it has been made into National Parks, so that people can enjoy it for years to come. The Peak District of Derbyshire has wild moorland and high peaks, while the Yorkshire Dales have gentler rolling hills. For hundreds of years, sheep have grazed on the Yorkshire moors, and their wool has been the raw material of most local industry. The Lake District, in Cumbria, is famous as the birthplace of the poet William Wordsworth.

Blackpool, in Lancashire, is famous for its illuminations – miles and miles of coloured lights.

The Brontë sisters, Anne, Charlotte and Emily, lived in Haworth, West Yorkshire.

JORVIK

The city of York is an ancient town,

ISLE OF MAN

The Isle of Man, off the west coast of northern England, has become very famous even though it is only a small island! Its TT motorcycle races draw crowds each year. Cats from the island, called Manx cats, can be recognized easily – they do not have tails!

▼ In Northumberland, during the time that the Romans were in Britain, the Emperor Hadrian had an enormous wall, stretching some 120km, built to keep northern tribes from attacking Roman settlements further south. Parts of Hadrian's wall can still be visited today.

full of beautiful, historic buildings. It was founded by the Vikings, who called it Jorvik. Today there are excellent exhibitions of Viking York, and a museum called the Jorvik Centre which brings ancient history to life. In the Middle Ages when the cathedral and many churches were built, York became one of the religious centres of England.

Eureka! is the name of an exciting Science Museum in Halifax, West Yorkshire.

TYNESIDE

Britain has a great seafaring history and many famous ships have been built and launched on Tyneside, on the east coast of northern England. At one time, some 25 per cent of all the world's shipping was built in Tyneside, although the industry is much smaller today.

WATERWAYS

When industry began to grow in northern England, roads were bad and horsedrawn vehicles very slow. To transport the goods that were manufactured, a vast network of canals was built. Now canals are used mainly for slow, leisurely holidays.

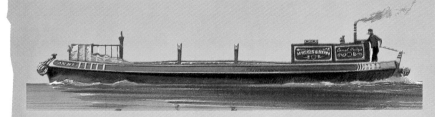

▼ The spectacular twin falls at Aysgarth in Wensleydale, North Yorkshire, are wide rather than high. The river falls over a series of limestone steps.

Scotland

WITH ITS MAGNIFICENT mountains and rolling lowlands, scattered islands and smart towns, Scotland is a land of contrasts.

England and Scotland have not always been friendly neighbours. Even after the two kingdoms were joined by the Act of Union of 1707 there was much bitter fighting. Cruel battles, such as Culloden in 1745, are still remembered.

Today, many Scots feel that Scotland should once again be more independent from England and in 1997 the people voted for a separate parliament.

THE BEANO IS PRINTED IN DUNDEE, A FEW WEEKS BEFORE IT REACHES YOU.

COLOUR

RRR PRINT HUMM

SO I CAN READ ABOUT WHAT'S GOING TO HAPPEN TO ME IN TWO WEEKS' TIME!

▲ Highland dancing in full traditional Scottish dress is still popular in Scotland.

RUNAWAY WEDDINGS

Gretna Green is famous as the place that eloping couples run away to so that they can be married without their parents' consent. Today, many marriages still take place in Gretna Green.

ANTARCTIC EXPLORER

In historic Dundee's harbour, you can visit famous ships from the past, including the *Discovery*, the ship in which Captain Scott set out for the Antarctic in 1901. Less than ten years later, he set out on another Antarctic expedition, but failed to return. Also in Dundee is the *Unicorn*, which is the oldest British warship still afloat. It was built in 1824.

Ben Nevis is the highest peak in Britain. So many people have climbed it that there is now a track all the way to the top!

Callanish standing stones on the Isle of Lewis date from the Bronze Age. It is said that they are giants, turned to stone!

▶ Cottages, such as this one in the Outer Hebrides, are often made from local stone, and then whitewashed. Thatching is still used for barn roofs.

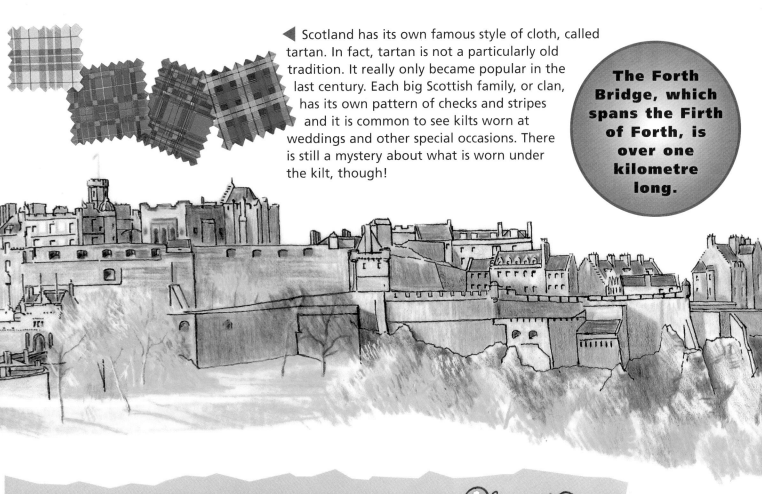

Scotland has its own famous style of cloth, called tartan. In fact, tartan is not a particularly old tradition. It really only became popular in the last century. Each big Scottish family, or clan, has its own pattern of checks and stripes and it is common to see kilts worn at weddings and other special occasions. There is still a mystery about what is worn under the kilt, though!

The Forth Bridge, which spans the Firth of Forth, is over one kilometre long.

MONSTERS OF THE DEEP

Scotland's geography means that its lakes, called lochs, are very deep. For many years there have been rumours that there is a 'monster' in Loch Ness. Many people believe that they have seen it, and extensive research, including surveys using sonar, has been carried out, but so far there has been no real proof.

Although it is built on hills and crags, Edinburgh is the very elegant capital of Scotland. Every year, the Edinburgh Festival brings thousands of visitors to see the plays and performances shown all over the city.

EDINBURGH BUILDINGS

Scott's Monument

Outlook Tower

John Knox's House

St Giles Cathedral

Wales

WALES HAS BEEN linked with England for hundreds of years, but the Welsh people are keen to keep their own customs and language. Farming, fishing and small industries are now the main employment as many of the coal mines that once filled the valleys have been closed down.

The Welsh celebrate their language and culture at festivals called Eisteddfods.

PRINCE OF WALES

Wales is not a kingdom – it is a principality. The heir to the British throne is usually given the title of Prince of Wales, marking the historic importance of this small country.

WELSH LANGUAGE

Road signs in Wales are given in Welsh and English, and the Welsh language is one of the oldest in the British Isles. The Welsh for Wales is Cymru, pronounced CUMree.

▲ The daffodil is a symbol of Wales. Many Welsh people wear a daffodil on St. David's Day.

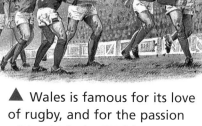

▲ Wales is famous for its love of rugby, and for the passion with which the Welsh support their team.

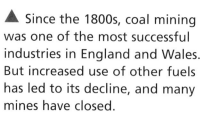

▲ Since the 1800s, coal mining was one of the most successful industries in England and Wales. But increased use of other fuels has led to its decline, and many mines have closed.

▲ Steam trains have been restored and are still working at the Talyllyn Railway on the north coast of Wales.

WHAT A GREAT BIG EGG!

THIS IS WALES! IT'S A RUGBY BALL!

WHUMP

Northern Ireland

THE SOUTHERN part of Ireland gained independence from the United Kingdom in 1921, leaving Northern Ireland as part of Britain. The division of Ireland has been the cause of much of the trouble that has developed there in recent years. Some Northern Irish people want to stay as part of Britain and others want to become part of Eire, the south.

Northern Ireland has a great tradition of folk music. Irish harps, bagpipes and fiddles are popular.

BELFAST

Shipbuilding and ropemaking were the industries of Belfast, Northern Ireland's capital. Today a third of Northern Ireland's population lives there.

THE SIX COUNTIES

Northern Ireland is divided into Londonderry, Antrim, Fermanagh, Armagh, Tyrone and Down. In Armagh, there is a huge mound called Navan Fort, which was the capital of the ancient kings of Ulster from 700BC.

▲ The red hand on the Northern Irish flag comes from an old story. It tells of how an Irish chieftain determined to win a race with a rival across a lough, or lake, cut off his hand and flung it on shore, so that he would be the first to 'touch' land.

▼ In rural areas, many houses are built low to the ground, to provide some shelter from the winds.

I'M AT THE GIANT'S CAUSEWAY. DON'T SEE ANY GIANTS!

HEH! HEH!

◀ The extraordinary natural pavement called the Giant's Causeway can be found on the northeast coast of Northern Ireland. It was formed when a volcanic rock called basalt cooled into hexagonal (six-sided) columns.

Minnie the Minx

BRITAIN'S A FUNNY PLACE TO LIVE, READERS — SEE WHAT IT'S DONE TO MY DAD!

HE'S ALWAYS GOING ON ABOUT THE WEATHER — IT GIVES ME A CHANCE TO MINX HIM!

THEN —

HURRY, MIN! WE'LL BE LATE FOR THE KICK-OFF!

YOU'RE USELESS, UNITED! TAKE UP CRICKET! SACK THE MANAGER!

IN THE AFTERNOON, DAD DRINKS TEA!

SUGAR, DAD? SPIDER, DAD?

ARGH! I HATE SPIDERS!

SHE'S EATEN MY SAUSAGES! THAT DOES IT!

HAHAHAHAHA!

DAD'S FLIPPED!

Britain at Play

BRITONS KNOW how to play hard as well as work hard and the British interest in sport is well known. For others, a night at the theatre is just as entertaining.

A SPORTING LIFE

Often thought of as the most British of games, cricket is also played in many parts of the world where Britons settled in the past. Each year, England plays different countries in a series of games called Test Matches.

One of the most famous tennis tournaments is held on the grass courts at Wimbledon. The world's best players come to London for the competition. Others remember it best for the strawberries and cream that are always served... whatever the weather!

Scotland is the home of golf. The course at St Andrews is one of the best known in the world.

▲ Some parts of Britain are well known for a particular instrument. In Wales and parts of Ireland, the harp is a traditional instrument. In Scotland, the famous bagpipes are played.

MAD ABOUT ANIMALS

The British are known to be mad about animals. Sports involving horses are specially popular. Some years ago Princess Anne competed for Britain in the Three Day Event at the Olympic Games.

DRAMATIC GESTURES

Many famous theatres are to be found in London and throughout the country. In recent years, musicals have been very popular, especially those by the British composer Andrew Lloyd Weber.

In the north of England, there are many excellent brass bands, that have grown up from factory or church music groups.

Wales is famous for its choirs and singers. A Welsh crowd singing at a rugby match is a wonderful sound – especially if Wales is winning!

Shakespeare's theatre, The Globe, has been rebuilt at its original site by the River Thames.

▲ Like cricket, football is played with two teams of 11 players. Every four years, teams from all over the world compete for the World Cup. England, Scotland and Ireland compete separately. England last won the World Cup in 1966.

Feasts and Festivals

MANY BRITISH celebrations, traditions and holidays come from religious festivals, sometimes dating back to before Christian times.

MORRIS DANCING

Traditional Morris dancers often wear bells on their shoes or legs. These days their dancing often seems to centre around public houses!

▶ In many parts of Britain, May Day is celebrated by dancing round a May Pole and choosing a May King and Queen. This is a very ancient custom dating from pre-Christian times.

LOW-FLYING PANCAKES!

In the Christian Church, the 40 days before Easter are called Lent. People used to fast during this time. This means that they went without food at certain times. Shrove Tuesday was the last day before Lent, so everyone ate as much as they could! Today, we make pancakes in memory of that and pancake races are held.

▲ At Easter, Christians celebrate Christ's rising from the dead. It's a time of new life. People give each other eggs, usually made of chocolate, to commemorate this.

BONFIRE NIGHT

November 5 is celebrated as Guy Fawkes' Night. The date commemorates when Guy Fawkes and other conspirators attempted to blow up the Houses of Parliament in 1605. A 'guy' is often burnt on a bonfire and there are firework displays in parks and gardens.

Can you spot the different foods the Beano kids are eating? Can you work out what they are celebrating?

GROAN! I HAVE TO COOK NINE DIFFERENT DISHES FOR NINE DIFFERENT KIDS!

CHRISTMAS IN OCTOBER!

It seems as though Christmas comes earlier every year as shops and streets are decorated in early autumn. Nearer to Christmas itself, carol singers visit homes or sing in the streets to collect money for charity. Every year in Trafalgar Square, a huge Christmas tree is set up, a present from the people of Norway.

▼ It is said that the Earl of Sandwich invented the snack which carries his name. The Earl was playing cards and did not want to stop to eat, so he put some meat between two pieces of bread.

THE NEW YEAR

In Scotland, Hogmanay (the New Year) is often celebrated more fully than Christmas. Here and in other parts of Britain, the ceremony of first footing is performed, where a dark stranger visits a house soon after midnight on January 1. This is supposed to ensure good luck throughout the year.

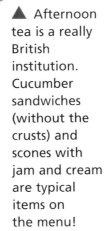

▲ Afternoon tea is a really British institution. Cucumber sandwiches (without the crusts) and scones with jam and cream are typical items on the menu!

THE GREAT BRITISH BREAKFAST

Britain is not widely known throughout the world for its food, but some things are too good to miss.

In many countries, a roll and coffee seems enough to start the day. A real British breakfast, however, has eggs, bacon, sausages, mushrooms, tomatoes, toast and marmalade – and several cups of tea!

FISH AND CHIPS

Where would we be without them? Almost every town has at least one fish and chip shop.

SCOTTISH SPECIALITIES

Oats were an important crop in Scotland in the past and today the Scots are still famous for their porridge and oatmeal biscuits. Another Scottish dish that contains oatmeal is haggis, although many people prefer not to know the other ingredients of this meat pudding – offal and onions, traditionally stuffed into a sheep's stomach! This delicacy is often served with neeps and chappit tatties (mashed swede and potatoes).

BREAD AND BUTTER PUDDING!

SLURP! PORRIDGE!

Nature in Britain

THE LANDSCAPE OF Britain is so varied that thousands of living things can find their own favourite habitats, or places to live. As well as species that live here all year, many birds migrate to Britain for just part of the year.

WOODLANDS

Hundreds of years ago, much of Britain was covered by huge forests of deciduous trees, which lose their leaves in winter. Today only a few ancient forests remain, but in recent years many new forests of conifers have been planted. Different creatures live in each kind of forest. The red squirrel, which prefers deciduous forests, is now quite rare, while the grey squirrel, which was introduced from North America, enjoys living in the new evergreen forests.

Sycamore

Acorn

Horse chestnut

Bluebell

Wood pigeon

Grey squirrel

Primrose

Badger

Yew

You could...
Ask a friend to help you hold a piece of paper against a tree trunk and rub evenly with a wax crayon. Make a collection of the patterns made by different kinds of bark.

DID YOU KNOW?

If you find a lot of broken snail shells near a large stone, it is probably a thrush's 'anvil'. This is where the thrush has crushed the shells on the stone to eat the snails inside.

In late spring and early summer, you will find broken eggshells lying beneath trees and hedges. By collecting the shells and looking them up in field guides, you can find out what kinds of birds have nested nearby.

Female blackbirds are not black – they are a dark brown colour.

All insects have six legs and three body parts. Anything with more legs, such as a spider or a centipede, is not an insect.

FARMLAND

Fields and hedgerows are home to many small creatures that can fit in with the farming year. In the past, many hedges were pulled up so that farmers could make bigger fields in which to use their large machinery. Now we realize just how important these hedgerows are.

A CAT! I'LL CHASE IT!

OOW! YELP! HOWL!

CORRECTION! WILDCAT!

Grasshopper

Rabbit

Fieldmouse

Brown butterfly

Cowslip

Hawthorn

MOUNTAINS AND HILLS

From the Highlands of Scotland to the rolling hills of the Yorkshire Dales, Britain provides homes for many living things that thrive on the often harsh conditions of high ground. Some hills are almost bare of plants, giving few places for small creatures to hide from their enemies. Other slopes are covered with forests, where larger animals, such as deer, can find homes.

Peregrine falcon

Red kite

Mountain hare

Red deer

Thistle

Wild cat

TOWNS AND CITIES

We think of towns and cities as being made up of buildings. In fact, there are lots of parks and gardens too, which give green spaces where plants and animals can live. Some countryside animals, such as foxes, are now finding that dustbins are an easier place to find food than the hedgerows!

▼ Whether you have a large garden or just a windowbox, you will be amazed at how much wildlife there is to be seen. It is easy to encourage more living things by putting out food and water when they are scarce in nature.

You could...
Make a bird table to attract birds to your garden in the winter. All you need is a flat, level surface positioned somewhere where it is not too easy for cats to reach it. Food can be put on the surface or hung from a post in the centre. Seeds, nuts, fat and water are all very welcome to hungry birds in bad weather. Be sure to put the bird table where you can see it from a nearby window.

Swift

Blackbird

Song thrush

Blue tit

Ladybird

Snail

Spider

Earthworm

Bumble bee

Slug

68

I'M A BIRD!

WHAT'S FOR DINNER, MUM?

HERE'S YOUR BREAD, BIRDIE!

SQUAWK!

PONDS AND RIVERS

Ponds and rivers have different wildlife, depending on whether the water is flowing. Often the level of water may change a great deal throughout the year. Always visit the water's edge with an adult as banks can be slippery and the water deep.

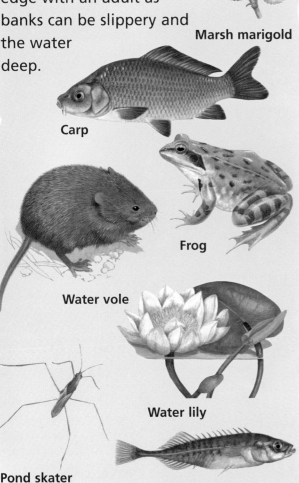

Marsh marigold

Carp

Water vole

Frog

Water lily

Pond skater

Stickleback

THE SEASHORE

The British Isles, of course, are surrounded by sea, and offer a home to an enormous number of creatures. When the tide recedes, mud flats are full of shellfish which provide food for many birds. Cliffs and rocks provide nesting sites. But seashore life is very hard. Plants need to be strong to be able to cope with salt water and strong winds.

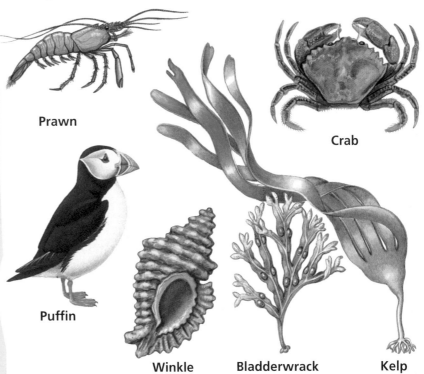

Prawn

Crab

Puffin

Winkle

Bladderwrack

Kelp

The Great British

BRITAIN HAS had many colourful and eccentric characters throughout its history. Here are just a few of them.

KINGS AND QUEENS

King Canute lived in the 11th century and is said to have ordered the sea to retreat. This makes him sound very silly, but he may have been trying to show his followers that even he could not work miracles!

▶ **Henry VIII**'s first divorce caused a disagreement with the Pope. Finally, Henry broke away from the Roman Catholic Church and was responsible for the beginnings of the Church of England.

◀ Unlike her father, Henry VIII, **Elizabeth I** never married. But she had a long and successful reign, during which Spanish invaders were successfully defeated. After her death in 1603, the two kingdoms of England (with Wales) and Scotland were united under James I.

▶ **Charles I** was executed and for a while after his death, Britain became a Commonwealth, with no monarch. Even to this day, some people remember the King's death in 1649 by laying flowers in Whitehall, London, each year.

Queen Victoria is Britain's longest reigning monarch so far. She ruled Britain for 64 years at the time when the British Empire was at its height. After the death of her husband, Albert, she became rather prim and sad, but later returned to public life and was often amused!

Mary, Queen of Scots was the mother of James I of England. Her name was linked to a plot against Elizabeth I and she was executed in 1587.

GREAT BRITISH HEROES

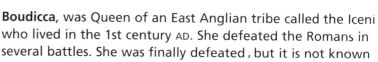

▶ **David Livingstone** was a Scottish missionary and explorer in the 19th century. He is now most often remembered not for his own words but for those of Henry Stanley who found him in the middle of Africa and greeted him with the words, "Dr Livingstone, I presume?".

Boudicca, was Queen of an East Anglian tribe called the Iceni who lived in the 1st century AD. She defeated the Romans in several battles. She was finally defeated, but it is not known where she is buried.

◀ **Winston Churchill** was Britain's great Prime Minister in World War II. He became a symbol of courage and persistance against enormous odds.

▼ **Horatio Nelson** was a great naval leader who lost both an arm and an eye fighting for his country. He once famously put a telescope to his blind eye and said, "I see no ships!" when he wanted to ignore an order.

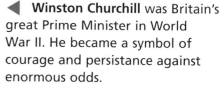

Scott of the Antarctic was a famous explorer. He struggled to reach the South Pole, only to find that the Norwegian explorer, Roald Amundson had reached there five weeks earlier! Although he died on his last expedition, he is still seen as a symbol of British courage and determination.

Hall of Fame

THIS IS MY HALL OF FAME!

FIRST JERSEY

BROKE TEN WINDOWS

LOANED BY WALTER

GNASHER'S PUPPY TOOTH

DAD'S SLIPPERS

HEROES OF FACT AND FICTION

◀ King Arthur may have been a 6th-century knight who helped defeat some Saxon invaders. Or he may have been a fictional character invented at a time when Britain needed a hero.

▶ Robin Hood stole from the rich to give to the poor, or did he? In fact, not much is really known about him, but it makes an exciting story. It could be that Robin Hood is based on the lives of several different people.

◀ Sherlock Holmes is so famous as the detective in the stories written by Sir Arthur Conan Doyle that every year many letters to him are received at 221B Baker Street in London – even though there's no such address!

SPORTING HEROES

Red Rum, one of Britain's most successful racehorses, was a great favourite with the public. When he died, he was buried by the winning post at Aintree, where he had some of his greatest successes.

Eddie the Eagle came to fame not for success but for trying – and failing! As a ski jumper, he had difficulties because he had to train in his back garden – without any snow!

Roger Bannister was the first man in the world to run a mile in under 4 minutes, back in 1954.

Frank Bruno is a former heavyweight champion boxer. He is so popular with the public that he has performed in pantomime and is regularly in television quiz shows.

And, of course, you may recognize this famous crew!

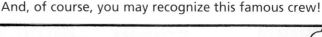

MISLEADING NAMES

John O'Groats, the name of the most northerly point of the British mainland isn't Scottish! It comes from Jan de Groot, a Dutchman!

Pill-boxes have nothing to do with pills! They are low, concrete buildings built as look-out posts during World War II.

Rotten Row is a place in Hyde Park, London, where horses can be ridden. But you don't need to hold your nose! The word comes from the French Route du Roi – the King's Road.

DID YOU KNOW?

▶ There were no towns at all in Britain until the Romans came. Before that, there were small village settlements.

▶ In the Victoria and Albert Museum, in London, you can see the Great Bed of Ware. It was made for an inn in Ware and it is so big that at least eight people could sleep in it at once!

▶ When the Queen is staying at Buckingham Palace, she has bagpipes played outside her apartments as she eats breakfast!

▶ The four bronze lions in Trafalgar Square were made of metal from cannon used in battle.

DID YOU KNOW?

▶ Britain's Union Flag has three crosses on it: the red cross of St George (for England), the diagonal blue cross of St Andrew (for Scotland) and the diagonal red cross of St Patrick (for Ireland). England and Scotland's flags were joined in 1710 and Ireland's was added in 1801.

AMAZING FACTS

The biggest lake in Britain is **Lough Neagh**, in Northern Ireland.

The longest river in Britain is the **River Severn,** which flows from the Midlands to the Bristol Channel.

The tallest spire in Britain is on **Salisbury Cathedral.** It is 123 metres high!

The highest mountain in Britain is **Ben Nevis**, in Scotland. It rises 1,343 metres above sea level.

Facts and Records

THINGS TO LOOK OUT FOR

▶ Old buildings with blocked-up windows. This was because of a window tax which ended in 1851. People blocked up their windows rather than pay the tax.

▶ Stubs of iron on top of walls. These are the remains of iron railings which were removed and used to make weapons in World War II.

▶ Pillar boxes. Some date from the Victorian period. These are often six-sided and have the letters VR on them.

DID YOU KNOW?

▶ Bollards, used in the street to stop vehicles parking on the pavement or going down a blocked street, were first made of an upturned cannon with a cannonball popped in the top!

▶ London's smallest police office is in Trafalgar Square. It is hidden in a small hollow pillar and has room for just one police officer!

▶ The most easterly point on the British mainland is in Lowestoft, Suffolk – at the very end of the pier!

▶ St George, the patron saint of England, was not British at all! He originally came from the Middle East.

AMAZING PLACE NAMES

The name of a place often gives clues to its original settlers. Do any of these words appear in the names of towns and villages near to where you live?

Roman place names
camp = plain
caster, cester, chester = fortified place
eccles = church
port = harbour

Anglo-Saxon place names
burg, borough, bury = fortified place
den, dene = valley
ea, ey = river
feld, field = field
ford = shallow river crossing
ham = settlement, home
head = hill
holt = dense wood
ing = people
lea, leigh, ley = clearing
mere = lake
sted, stead = place
stoke, stow = meeting place
ton, tun = farm or village
wald = wood
wic, wick, wich = farm
worth = hedged land

Viking place names
by = village
thorpe = small village
toft = farmstead

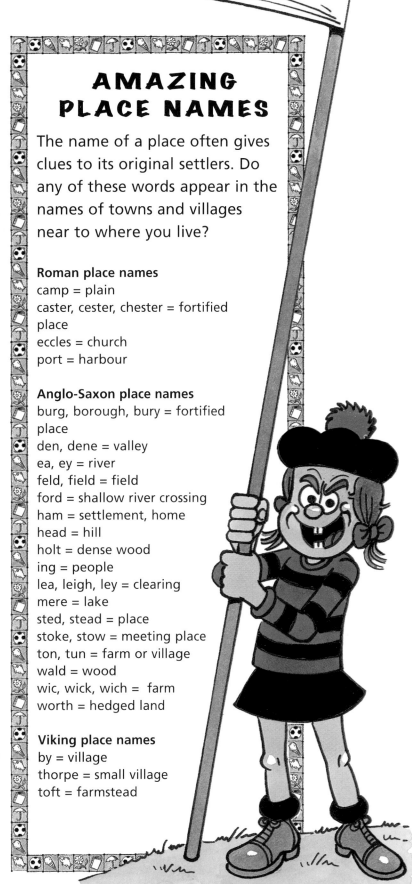

VOTE FOR THE TEACHER PARTY — MORE HOMEWORK, HARDER SUMS!

BOO!

VOTE FOR THE KIDS PARTY — 53 WEEKS HOLIDAY A YEAR!

IT'S VOTING TIME!

TEACHER PARTY, TWO VOTES!

YOU IDIOT, SMIFFY!

...ES, SIR, HEADMASTER, SIR!

DAFT TEACHER

AS PRIME MINISTER I GIVE MYSELF A DAY OFF!

NOW THAT I'M IN CHARGE OF THE KIDS PARTY...

...I'LL MAKE JELLY FOR THE PARTY!

BOP

SOCK!

CRUNCH

TO THE FIRST AID ROOM WITH THIS LOT!

GROAN!

AS PRIME MINISTER, I HOPE YOU'VE ENJOYED THIS SUPERB BOOK!

VOTE MICE

Index

Photographic credits: 41 Peter Newark; 50 both photos Doug Baird Department of Tourism and Leisure, Isle of Man; 51 Yorkshire and Humberside Tourist Board.